THE UNITED NATIONS OF
COOKIES

Jess Murphy & Eoin Cluskey

To Heather

Enjoy all the
baked Cookies
♡x Jess

BLASTA

CONTENTS

INTRODUCTION

JESS

I didn't know it at the time, but for me, the idea for this book started when I was standing on a hill just outside of Amman in Jordan, overlooking the Azraq refugee camp. I had just flown out on my first mission for the UNHCR, the United Nations Refugee Agency, in 2019. I was heading to Beirut and Jordan to document Syrian food history through displacement and to meet the Al Jamous family (who contributed the wonderful Syrian cookie recipe on page 48), who were living in a tiny apartment in Beirut and had just received the good news that they were about to be relocated to Ireland. It was the most heart-warming experience I've ever had. We had Fattie and John Burkes' book, Irelandopedia, open, looking for their new country, their new home. My husband, David, managed to get his phone working and we watched the hurling highlights with 11-year-old Mohamed, who didn't know where Ireland was.

We did our best to reassure the family that they were going to be safe and that Sami's dream of his kids being able to ride a bicycle in the fresh air on the street outside would indeed come true. We promised to come see them, but little did we know that they were going to live just up the road in County Offaly. It was a humbling experience that showed me how small the world is and how important empathy and understanding are in these situations. Catching the train to Offlay to be reunited and pop in for a cuppa was just magic.

I still remember something that a mother in the Bekaa Valley in Lebanon said to me about her eight-year-old son – she told me that her only hope for getting out of their situation was his education, as it would determine the future of the family. He wanted to be an architect and to build a beautiful house for his mother. I hope with all my heart they get there. It was a stark contrast from my upbringing in New Zealand in the 1980s, where my biggest problem was that fish and chips Friday couldn't come soon enough. Her words have stayed with me ever since.

COOKIES & CONNECTIONS
Back in 2019, we had a crazy idea for a milk-and-cookies show that we could take on the road to schools all around the country. Eoin has an old milk float that would have been perfect for it and I'm a one-woman aficionado on proper Irish milk, the liquid

gold full-fat sunniness that our farmers produce with love and care on lush green fields. Between my work with UNHCR and Eoin being the most amazing Cookie Master, we knew we could pull it off. Then the covid pandemic shut everything down.

But then we had another idea, one that brought me back to that moment on the hilltop in Jordan – what if we collected a cookie recipe from refugees and immigrants who we know in Ireland and put them in a book? It would still give us a chance to talk about the importance of culture and what it means to us – that it's delicious, it's exciting and it comes in every colour, shape and size, just like me and you. It would be a way to highlight how deadly it is to be different and unique and to always strive to be your best self and to take pride in where you come from.

These cookies are a symbol for the changing face of Ireland – the Ireland that has become a safe haven and home for so many, including myself and my big love for all things Galway – while still keeping the traditional Ireland that we adore close to our hearts.

This book has been a catalyst for community connections and has been grounding for both myself and Eoin. It has sparked conversations with those around us on a level that neither of us could have imagined. Over the past year, we have heard so many beautiful stories from people like Aunty Susan (who shared her Persian rice cookie on page 40) and Izz and Eman (check out their maamoul on page 38), which you will get to read in this book. These are recipes that have been passed from generation to generation, made for everything from your lunchbox to traditional holidays and anything in between. It's been a privilege to listen, learn and connect.

EOIN

Food has an innate and inspiring power. We share recipes, we bake, then we come together to enjoy the reward of the work we have done. There is satisfaction and pride in using our hands to bake something, but specifically in this book, to bake cookies.

I grew up baking in my grandmother's kitchen, drawn to the waft of real bread or cookies coming from the oven. Now, many years later, when I take a bite of something freshly baked, I am transported back to those days. For many of us, that first bite of a cookie is a not just delicious taste of something, but also a powerful prompt back to memories of the different cookies we've had before or maybe ones we've made with methods that are traditional to other countries. The beauty of this is what this book is all about.

This book has given Jess and I the chance to share recipes from all over the world from extraordinary people. In those conversations exchanging recipes and ideas, we were transported to the places that the people we met called home before they made their new home in Ireland. In this book, my food vision, Jess's food vision and the vision of the contributors of these recipes come together as one voice. Everyone should have the chance to share their perspective when it comes to food, and what is more universal, more joyful and more celebrated than a simple cookie?

COMMUNITY & CREATIVITY

As I grew up, I went down different paths such as travelling and carpentry until I found my way back to baking. Along the way, I fell in love with real bread and real food. Today, my business, Bread 41 – an organic bakery, café and eatery in the heart of Dublin – has grown to build a community of people eating real bread and prioritising its benefits over industrialised bread. We also encourage education around using what the earth creates – of foraging, pickling, fermenting, etc. Beyond that and the artisan pastries sold daily, it has grown to build a community following our 'Move to Zero'. This is our journey to becoming fully zero waste and recognising the importance of being a sustainability-centric business, of the power of buying into it as a concept that our customers can then apply at home. Similar to the message we're trying to promote with this book, we try to encourage people to see food as a global concept and see its impact not just in terms of creativity, but also in terms of waste and production, as something with global consequences.

This project is hugely aligned with the strong values that make Bread 41 the success it has been. Like this book, it's about community and the creativity of food made the right way, by anyone. It's about bringing people from different cultures together to work on the shared purpose of ethically creating food that brings joy. Team 41 continues to grow as a team of many nationalities, with everyone bringing their own ideas to the table. Caring for others and their voices is the business's primary value.

With this book, I want our community and beyond to see the impact that food and sharing what food means to us and to others can have. We can rekindle that childhood nostalgia, that simplicity and joy of food, while addressing the challenges our world faces and the need to come together. At its core, food is universal and ever evolving. This book is a love letter to how it brings us all together.

AFGHANI SHORTBREAD
NANKHATAI

MAKES 20

KHATIRA HASSANPOUR – These cookies are very popular in Afghanistan. They remind me of my parents, as we ate them all the time when we were children, especially on New Year's Eve. My mom still makes them at home.

250ml sunflower or vegetable oil, gently warmed

120g icing sugar

1 tsp ground cardamom

1 tsp vanilla extract

300g plain flour

50g pistachios, very finely chopped

Put the warm oil and icing sugar in a large bowl and mix until well combined and smooth. Add the cardamom and vanilla and mix again.

Add the flour and mix with a wooden spoon or gently knead with your hands until the mixture comes together into a soft, smooth dough.

Place the dough in a bowl, cover with cling film and chill in the fridge for 1 hour to firm up.

Preheat the oven to 150°C fan. Line two baking trays with non-stick baking paper.

Using a tablespoon, scoop out small balls of the dough, roll them into neat balls between the palms of your hands and place on the lined baking trays, spaced a little bit apart. Press each dough ball lightly with your finger to put a little dent in the top (to sprinkle the pistachios into after baking).

Bake in the oven for 20 minutes. Remove from the oven and add a pinch of chopped pistachios into the indent you made in each cookie. Allow to cool for 10 minutes on the trays, then transfer to a wire rack to cool completely.

AFGHANISTAN

KHATIRA HASSANPOUR

Khatira grew up in Iran, but her family fled in 1984 during the Soviet invasion of Afghanistan. Four decades later, the subsequent waves of violence and displacement from Afghanistan continue in what is now the longest protracted refugee situation covered under UNHCR's mandate. Today, Iran is host to over 3 million Afghans. Khatira, a translator by profession, now lives in Galway with her husband and two children.

Like Afghan refugees in Iran, she preserves the taste of home with food such as nankhatai, a type of shortbread biscuit. 'I used to watch my mom cook them all the time with my aunt and grandmother, sitting with each other preparing them for New Year,' Khatira says. 'It's not difficult to make, but following the recipe is important, so pay attention to the oil and sugar.'

LIKE AFGHAN REFUGEES IN IRAN, KHATIRA PRESERVES THE TASTE OF HOME WITH FOOD SUCH AS NANKHATAI, A TYPE OF SHORTBREAD BISCUIT.

AMERICAN MONSTER COOKIES

MAKES 18–20

HANNAH O'DONNELL – I grew up in a small town called New Braintree in Massachusetts. My mom is also a chef and I remember her coming into my school and teaching my class how to make pizza, egg rolls and, best of all, cookies. I love this cookie recipe because you can put all your favourite candy in the dough or use up what's in the cupboard or left over from Halloween or Easter. I like salty bits in my chocolate chip cookies, so I add pretzels. These also freeze really well, so you can have a batch ready to go anytime you need that sweet 'n' salty fix.

170g unsalted butter, softened

220g soft brown sugar

80g caster sugar

1 large egg

2 tsp vanilla extract

225g plain flour

2 tsp flaky sea salt

½ tsp baking soda

150g dark chocolate chips

100g peanut M&Ms

4 Reese's Peanut Butter Cups, roughly chopped

a handful of pretzels, roughly broken or chopped

a handful of pecans

Cream together the butter and sugars in a large bowl until light and fluffy. Add the egg and vanilla and mix again until fully combined. Add the flour, salt and baking soda and mix until just combined into a dough.

Using your hands, work in the chocolate chips, peanut M&Ms, peanut butter cups, pretzels and pecans until evenly distributed.

Divide the dough into roughly 55g or ¼ cup portions and roll into balls. Place on a plate, cover with cling film and chill in the fridge for at least 1 hour, until firm. This dough will keep in the fridge for up to five days or in the freezer for three months.

Preheat the oven to 180°C fan. Line two baking trays with non-stick baking paper.

Place the chilled balls of dough on the lined trays, spaced well apart. Bake in the oven for about 15 minutes, until golden brown and baked through.

Remove from the oven and allow to cool on the trays for about 5 minutes, until they've firmed up a bit, before transferring to a wire rack to cool completely.

BRAZILIAN SNACK BISCUITS
BISCOITO DE POLVILHO

MAKES A FEW DOZEN, DEPENDING ON SIZE

FABIANO MAYOR – These savoury biscuits are cheap and filling, almost like popcorn, and you'll find them all over Brazil. They use tapioca flour, which is abundant and traditional in South American countries. Tapioca flour is how you're most likely to find it sold in Ireland at Asian markets, but some people say yuca, some people say cassava and some people say manioc. It's all the same thing, but no matter what you call it, it must be very white and very fine, like powder.

180ml water, plus another 100ml

70ml vegetable oil

450g tapioca flour

1 tsp fine sea salt

1 egg, beaten well

Preheat the oven to 200°C fan.

Put 180ml of water and the vegetable oil in a small saucepan and bring to the boil, then pour into a heatproof jug.

Put the tapioca flour and salt in a large bowl and mix to combine. Slowly drizzle in the hot water and oil a little bit at a time, mixing with a metal spoon. Once it has all been added, use your hands to rub the mixture into the consistency of fine breadcrumbs.

Add the beaten egg. Still using your hands, work it into the flour. It will start to form large clumps. Drizzle in the remaining 100ml of water one tablespoon at a time. With your hand in a claw shape (like you would do for mixing soda bread), mix the water into the flour. Keep adding the water a little at a time until the dough is smooth and has the consistency of choux pastry dough – it should be thick and firm and can hold its shape, but it should also still be runny enough to fall off a spoon after a few seconds. You might not need all of the 100ml of water or you might need a little more.

Spoon the dough into a piping bag with a plain nozzle or a large ziplock bag with the tip snipped off. Pipe the dough into rings directly on two unlined baking trays. They won't spread, so you can pipe them close together.

TRY THIS

Some versions add 50g of finely grated Parmesan and some dried oregano.

Bake in the oven for about 15 minutes, until the bottoms are starting to get golden and the biscuits are crisp. Allow to cool on wire racks.

BRITISH JAMMY DODGERS

MAKES 12

ALICE JARY – I'm from King's Lynn in Norfolk. I moved to Ireland when I was pretty young, but I have memories of driving up the east coast of England past the lavender fields with my nan and grandad to go strawberry picking. You paid for a punnet and you got to choose the juiciest strawberries you could find. This, coupled with my love for the produce in Ireland – like the amazing strawberries we have here in the summer – is why I love this recipe.

250g plain flour, plus extra for dusting

30g cornflour

60g icing sugar

220g salted butter, diced and chilled

2 egg yolks, beaten

caster sugar, for sprinkling

your favourite jam (I use strawberry jam from McCambridge's in Galway)

Mix the flours and icing sugar in a large bowl, then rub in the butter until the mix resembles breadcrumbs. Make a well in the centre, then pour in the egg yolks.

Using your hands, mix from the inside out, gathering the flour as you go. Stop mixing as soon as the dough comes together into a ball to make sure your biscuits are nice and crumbly once baked. Form the dough into a disc, wrap it in cling film and refrigerate for at least 30 minutes.

Line two baking trays with non-stick baking paper.

Roll out the dough on a lightly floured surface until it's 5mm thick. Using a round cookie cutter, stamp out the cookies and place on the lined trays. Gather the remaining dough into a ball, roll it out again and repeat.

Using a small heart-shaped cutter, stamp hearts out of the centres of half of the circles. Sprinkle caster sugar over the unbaked cookies and return to the fridge for 30 minutes more.

Preheat the oven to 175°C fan.

Bake the cookies in the oven for 12–15 minutes, until light golden. Remove from the oven and leave on the trays to set and cool completely.

Once cooled, spread a generous amount of jam on the plain, unstamped cookies, then sandwich them together with the biscuits with the hearts and gently press them together.

CANADIAN FAT ARCHIES

MAKES 12–15

JANINE KENNEDY – On my home island of Cape Breton on the east coast of Canada, there are numerous names for these thick, chewy molasses cookies. In my community we call them fat archies, but no one really knows where the name comes from. Molasses is a staple ingredient in any Cape Bretoner's diet. We pour it on our pork, drizzle it on biscuits (scones) when they're hot out of the oven and, of course, we bake with it all the time. My Aunt Helen is arguably the best cook in our family and this is her recipe. She always has a recipe to share if I'm craving a taste of home.

200g unsalted butter, softened

250g granulated sugar

1 large egg

1 tsp vanilla extract

1 tbsp baking soda

150ml hot tea

300g black treacle or molasses

700g plain flour, plus extra for dusting

1 tsp fine sea salt

1 tsp cream of tartar

½ tsp ground ginger

½ tsp ground cinnamon (optional)

Cream together the butter and sugar until pale and fluffy. Add the egg and vanilla and mix again until evenly combined.

Stir the baking soda into the hot tea. Add the treacle or molasses to the butter and sugar mixture, then add the hot tea mixture slowly to temper the egg. Mix until well combined. It might look curdled or grainy at this point, but don't worry, it will all work out.

Sift the flour, salt, cream of tartar, ginger and cinnamon (if using) over the top of the wet ingredients. Mix until well combined – the dough will be wet and sticky, more like a thick cake batter than cookie dough at this point. Cover the bowl with cling film and chill in the fridge overnight.

The next day, preheat the oven to 150°C fan. Line two baking trays with non-stick baking paper.

Generously dust a work surface with flour. Roll out the chilled dough until it's roughly 3cm thick (yes, really!) and stamp out with a large round cutter (or use a wine glass).

Bake in the oven for about 25 minutes. Don't overbake them – their colour won't change much once they're baked, but they should be well-risen. Allow to cool on a wire rack, then store in an airtight container for up to a week. They are amazing with a hot cup of tea, and while this isn't traditional, they also make fantastic ice cream sandwiches.

BAKER'S NOTE

Lightly grease a small bowl with sunflower or vegetable oil, then tare your scale to zero and pour in the treacle or molasses – it will slide right out of the bowl.

DUTCH LEMON & FENNEL CRINKLE COOKIES

MAKES 6 DOZEN

YVETTE VAN BOVEN – I was raised in Ireland but moved back to Holland when I was 10, though I still come back to my holiday home in West Cork. I loved to bake cookies when I was a child. It was something you could do by yourself and they were usually finished in the same afternoon. I enjoyed the baking part even more than the eating part! I think that's why I became a cook later on in life – baking has always been my favourite thing to do.

These cookies are deliciously lemony. Their cores are soft and the edges are crisp – real binge-eat biscuits. My husband, Oliver, is a Cookie Monster and he loves these. Sometimes I make them with freshly grated ginger, cracked black pepper or crushed dried lavender instead of the fennel seeds, but ground cardamom works well too. I dare you to try your own combo.

225g unsalted butter, softened, plus extra for greasing

225g granulated sugar

zest and juice of 1 lemon

1 tbsp fennel seeds, ground in a mortar and pestle

1 tsp vanilla extract

1 egg

300g plain flour

1 tsp baking powder

pinch of salt

100g icing sugar, sifted

Preheat the oven to 175°C fan. Grease two large baking trays or line with non-stick baking paper.

Beat the butter with the granulated sugar until light and airy. Add the lemon zest and juice, ground fennel seeds and vanilla, then beat in the egg.

Combine the flour, baking powder and salt, then use a spatula to stir the dry ingredients into the butter mixture to form a dough.

Pour the icing sugar into a deep plate or wide, shallow bowl.

Using a teaspoon, scoop out small portions of the dough. With wet hands, roll into balls the size of large grapes. Roll them through the icing sugar and space them generously (say, 5cm) apart on the baking trays.

Bake in the oven only briefly, about 8 minutes. Keep an eye on them so that they don't get overbaked and lose their chewiness. Cool on a wire rack.

Store the cookies in a large airtight container, where they'll keep for at least a week.

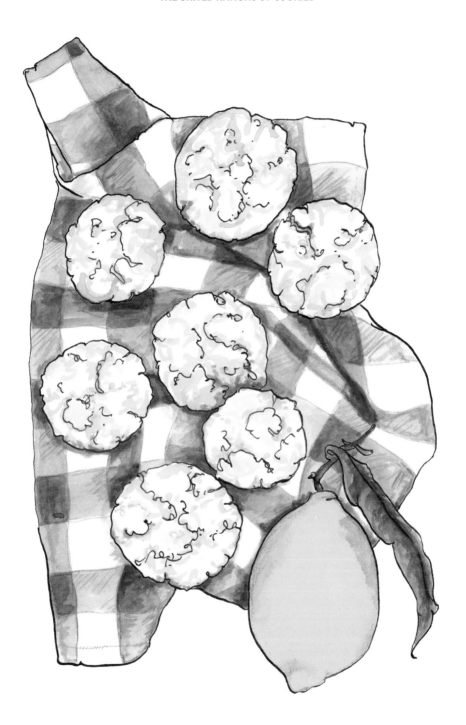

FINNISH SPOON COOKIES
LUSIKKALEIVÄT

MAKES 18

MICKAEL VILJANEN – These are my favourite cookies. Both my mother and grandmother used to make them in Finland, so I grew up on them. I ate them after school dinner on Thursdays, after our pea soup and pancakes.

200g unsalted butter, diced

125g caster sugar

1 vanilla pod, halved lengthways and seeds scraped out

300g plain flour

1 tsp baking soda

FOR THE FILLING:

100g stiff raspberry jam

FOR THE TOPPING:

caster sugar, for rolling

First you need to brown the butter, so put it in a heavy-based saucepan over a medium heat and whisk it often. Once it has melted it will foam up, but then it will stop bubbling. You'll see brown specks starting to form on the bottom of the pan and it will start to smell nutty. Once it has turned a golden-brown colour, remove the pan from the heat and stir in the sugar and vanilla seeds.

While the butter is browning, preheat the oven to 180°C fan. Line two baking trays with non-stick baking paper.

Mix the flour and baking soda together, then sift this into the butter and sugar mixture in the pan.

Press a small ball of the dough into the well of a small spoon, then carefully pop it out and put it on the lined baking trays, leaving a little space in between each quenelle. Repeat until you've used up all the dough.

Bake in the oven for 12–15 minutes, until light golden. Allow to cool completely on a wire rack.

Spread a little jam on the flat bottom of each cooled biscuit, then sandwich them together.

Put a good amount of caster sugar into a small bowl. Roll the sandwiched biscuits in the sugar to coat completely before serving.

GREEK EASTER COOKIES
KOULOURAKIA

MAKES 2 DOZEN

MARISSA MENELAOU – These cookies embody the essence of being Greek. We even have a nursery rhyme about them! Seeing them brings back memories of family and friends gathered around the table to make, bake and share them. Most Greek households only make them at Easter, when we make huge batches that would be shared with neighbours and friends. Now, however, you can buy them from Greek bakeries throughout the year, so our jars at home are filled with them all year round and many cafés serve them as a complimentary cookie with your coffee.

250g unsalted butter, softened

90g icing sugar

3 medium eggs

1 tbsp brandy or 1 tsp vanilla extract

2 heaped tsp baking powder

700–750g plain flour, plus extra for dusting

TO DECORATE:

1 egg, beaten

sesame seeds (optional)

Preheat the oven to 180°C fan. Line two large baking trays with non-stick baking paper.

Beat the butter and icing sugar together until light and fluffy. Add the eggs one at a time, beating well after each addition, then add the brandy or vanilla and the baking powder. It may look curdled at this point, but don't worry, it will be fine. Add the flour 100g at a time, mixing until you have a soft dough. It should not be sticky.

Dust your countertop or a board with a little flour. Break off a small piece of the dough (about 2 tablespoons or 50g of dough) and roll it into a ball between the palms of your hands, then roll it out on the lightly floured board into a 15cm-long rope. These are small biscuits meant to fit on an espresso saucer.

My favourite shape is a type of coiled letter S – coil one half of the strand down towards the middle of the rope, then coil the other half of the strand up in the opposite direction, meeting in the middle. Place on the lined trays, spaced well apart. Repeat with the remaining dough, playing around with different shapes if you like, such as a twisted plait or a figure 8 (you'll need to roll out the dough closer to 20cm for these).

Brush the tops with the beaten egg, then sprinkle with sesame seeds (if using). Bake in the oven for 20 minutes, until golden brown. Allow the biscuits to cool completely on the trays.

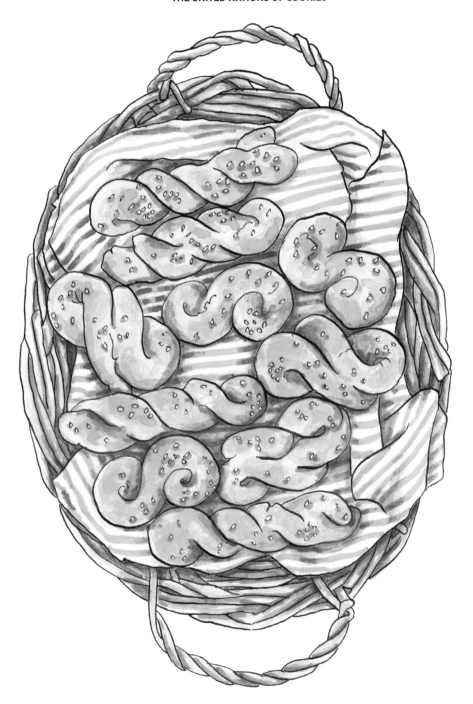

HONG KONG-STYLE EGG ROLL COOKIES

MAKES 10

KWANGHI CHAN – These cookies remind me of going to my aunties' house in Hong Kong when I was little, where tea was poured and the cookies were eaten during conversations with friends and family. There are many different varieties of bakes and biscuits in Hong Kong, from the simplest to more extravagant ones with fruit flavours or ginger or ones from stalls on the street where the bakers have spent their whole lives making recipes passed down for generations in their family business. I love to have these with Chinese green tea.

2 eggs

80g caster sugar

100g plain flour

¼ tsp fine sea salt

50g butter, melted, plus extra for greasing

black sesame seeds (optional)

Crack the eggs into a large mixing bowl and lightly beat with a whisk. Add the sugar and whisk until the sugar has dissolved and the mixture has turned light and increased a bit in volume.

Sift the flour and salt into the sugar and egg mixture and whisk until it's a smooth batter. Finally, whisk in the melted butter. Switch to a rubber spatula and stir again to make sure there are no pockets of flour in the batter.

Heat the egg roll/waffle cone maker over a medium heat. Open it up and brush both sides with a little melted butter. Add a heaped tablespoon of the batter to the middle of the pan, then sprinkle over some black sesame seeds (if using). Lower the lid, pressing it down lightly to spread out the batter. Cook for 20 seconds, then flip the pan over and cook for 20 seconds more. Do this a few more times, until the cookie is light golden brown on both sides. It might take one or two tries to get the hang of making the cookies, similar to the way the first pancake tends to never come out quite right. And because the cookies cook so quickly, this is not the time to be scrolling through your social media – trust me on that!

BAKER'S NOTE

You will need an egg roll/waffle cone maker to make these cookies. It's like a tortilla press that you can heat on the hob – you can find them online.

Working very quickly, while the cookie is still warm and pliable, roll it up as tightly as you can into a cigar shape – but be careful, the cookie will be very hot. Transfer to a wire rack to cool and firm up. Repeat with the remaining batter, brushing the egg roll/waffle cone maker with a little more butter before making each cookie.

INDIAN CHILLI & CORIANDER BISCUITS
KHARA

MAKES 4 DOZEN

MILIE MATHEW & SANTOSH THOMAS – We Indians love our sweet and savoury cookies. Santosh cherishes his memories of making mango burfi with his mother. As they did not have an oven, different types of burfi (a no-bake treat) were the go-to cookie in their household. Santosh would help to peel and slice the mangoes so that he could sneak some mango slices when his mother wasn't looking.

My father was an avid tea drinker and loved a masala cookie or a khara biscuit like the one given here with his sweet tea, so savoury cookies were made every week. I remember joining my mother in rolling out these cookies and cutting them into different shapes, but my favourite shape was a heart.

250g coarse wholewheat flour

250g plain flour

2 tbsp caster sugar

1 tsp fine sea salt

¼ tsp baking powder

¼ tsp baking soda

75g unsalted butter, melted

2 fresh green chillies, deseeded and finely chopped

10g fresh coriander leaves (a large handful), chopped

300g natural yogurt

Mix together the flours, sugar, salt, baking powder and baking soda in a large bowl. Add the melted butter, chopped green chillies and coriander leaves and stir until the mixture forms crumbs, then add the yogurt, bring the dough together gently and knead it once. Form it into a ball, then wrap it in cling film and chill it in the fridge for 30 minutes to firm up.

Preheat the oven to 180°C fan. Line two baking trays with non-stick baking paper.

Roll out the dough until it's 2mm thick and stamp out into circles using a cookie cutter, scone cutter or the rim of a glass. Place on the lined baking trays, spaced a little bit apart.

Bake in the oven for 15–18 minutes, until cooked through. Allow to cool on a wire rack, then serve with tea or coffee.

BAKER'S NOTE

Milie's father liked to have his khara with sweet tea, but we think these savoury biscuits would also be excellent with a sharp, mature Cheddar and a spoonful of mango chutney.

JAPANESE WASABI CREAM CHEESE COOKIES

MAKES 12

TAKASHI MIYAZAKI – In Japan, there are many savoury sweets – think chocolate-covered potato chips. My two boys, Seán and Stephen, don't eat wasabi, as it is too spicy for kids. But if you use it to make sweets like a cookie, then the spiciness is gone but the savoury flavour is still in the cookies. For example, you can buy seaweed, wasabi and Cheddar sandwich cookies or even a wasabi and Camembert version to have as a small bite with a beer in Japan. My boys love these.

100g unsalted butter, softened

100g caster sugar

300g plain flour

FOR THE WASABI CREAM CHEESE:

2 tbsp soy sauce

1 tbsp mirin

1 tbsp sake (optional)

100g cream cheese

1 tbsp wasabi paste (from a tube)

You need to make the wasabi cream cheese the day before you bake the cookies. Heat the soy sauce, mirin and sake (if using) in a small saucepan over a medium-high heat. When it's just starting to boil, take the pan off the heat and allow to cool.

Whisk together the cream cheese, wasabi and the cooled soy sauce mixture in a small bowl. Cover the bowl tightly with cling film and chill it in the fridge overnight.

The next day, take the wasabi cream cheese out of the fridge – you may need to whisk it again to combine.

Cream the butter and wasabi cream cheese together, then add the sugar and beat until light and fluffy. Add the flour and beat again until just combined. Cover the bowl with cling film and chill in the fridge for 1 hour.

Preheat the oven to 170°C fan. Line two baking trays with non-stick baking paper.

Portion out pieces of dough – each one should be about 2 tablespoons or 50g – and roll into a ball. Place each ball about 5cm apart on the lined trays.

Bake in the oven for 15–20 minutes, until the tops have cracked and the cookies are golden brown around the edges. Allow to cool on a wire rack.

BAKER'S NOTE

If you like wasabi peas, you'll love these!

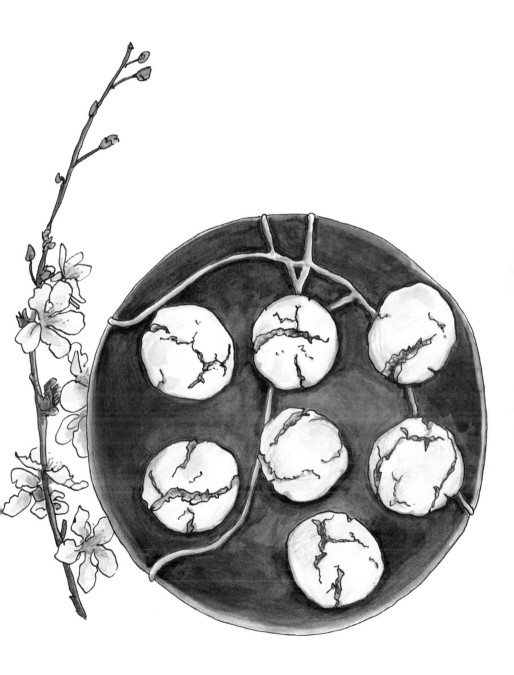

LITHUANIAN LAZY COOKIES
TINGINYS

MAKES 20 SLICES

EMILIJA JEFREMOVA – Since I live 2,000km from my mum, Audroné, in Lithuania and don't have a sweet tooth, she came up with a solution for a biscuit that travels well, is light and not too sweet. It is also very easy to make, as it's a no-bake cookie – in fact, 'tinginys' means lazy!

400g Gaidelis cookies or digestive biscuits

150g unsalted butter, melted

5 tbsp cocoa powder

1 x 400g tin of condensed milk

OPTIONAL EXTRAS:

nuts

dried fruit

chocolate chips or a chopped chocolate bar

Break the cookies or digestives into small pieces by hand and set aside in a bowl.

Whisk the melted butter and cocoa powder together in a large mixing bowl. Pour in the condensed milk and whisk again until it's well combined and completely smooth, then tip in the broken cookies or digestives and any optional extras. Using a spatula, gently fold them in until everything is evenly combined, making sure you're scraping up all the condensed milk mixture at the bottom of the bowl.

You can either scrape the mixture into a loaf tin, cake tin or square brownie tin lined with cling film, smoothing the top as best you can, or tip it out onto a large piece of cling film and roll it up into a log, twisting the ends to seal it in the cling film.

Chill in the fridge for at least 2 hours or overnight to let it firm up before cutting into slices to serve.

BAKER'S NOTE

When we made these, we formed it into a log roughly 28cm long and got 20 slices. It's a little sticky even after being chilled, so you might want to eat these cookies with a fork.

MALAYSIAN PEANUT BUTTER COOKIES
KUIH KACANG

MAKES 14

SHAMZURI (SHAM) HANIFA – These were the 'good' biscuits that my grandmother always gave me when I was a kid. At the time they were the most expensive ones and were usually reserved for special occasions. We would do anything to get them, so they were often used as bribes. I haven't been that good since!

225g blanched peanuts

225g plain flour

115g peanut butter

115g caster sugar

75ml sunflower oil

1 egg yolk, beaten

Preheat the oven to 180°C fan. Line two baking trays with non-stick baking paper.

Blitz the peanuts in a food processor until they are a coarse powder, but be careful not to blend them too much or they may start to turn into peanut butter.

Tip out into a large mixing bowl and stir in the flour, peanut butter and sugar. Slowly add the oil and mix until it comes together into a dough.

Tip the dough out onto the countertop and roll it out until it's 2cm thick. Stamp out the cookies using a round cookie cutter, scone cutter or the rim of a glass. Place on the lined baking trays, spaced a little bit apart – they won't spread very much. Brush the tops with the beaten egg yolk.

Bake in the oven for 12–15 minutes, until golden brown. Leave to cool on the trays for few minutes before serving these crumbly cookies with tea or coffee.

BAKER'S NOTE

We used our favourite Irish artisan peanut butter, Nut Shed, in these cookies. You can get blanched peanuts in Asian markets.

MEXICAN PIGLET COOKIES
MARRANITOS

MAKES 15

LILY RAMIREZ-FORAN – Marranitos, or piglets, are one of Mexico's most traditional cookies, sold in panaderias (bakeries) all over the country. When I was little, my granddad used to take me to the local panaderia and buy a few of these cookies for me and my sister. We would go back to the house carrying the cookies in a brown bag and have them with a big glass of cold milk as our merienda, which is the Mexican version of afternoon tea.

250g Mexican piloncillo, roughly chopped (or see the tip)

120ml water

1 Mexican cinnamon stick

3 cloves

1½ tsp aniseeds (the seeds, not ground)

700g plain flour, plus extra for dusting

180g icing sugar

1½ tsp baking powder

250g salted butter, chilled and cut into small cubes

2 medium eggs, beaten

FOR THE EGG WASH:

1 small egg

¼ tsp caster sugar

⅛ tsp fine sea salt

Put the piloncillo, water, cinnamon stick, cloves and aniseeds in a small saucepan over a medium heat and bring to a gentle boil. Lower the heat a little and let the piloncillo melt gently, stirring every now and then. Cook for 10–15 minutes, until the piloncillo has melted completely and you have a dark, fragrant, slightly runny syrup. Remove the pan from the heat and let it cool down. Once it's cool enough, remove the cinnamon stick and the whole cloves and set the syrup aside.

Sift the flour, icing sugar and baking powder into a large bowl and mix to combine. Add the cold butter and rub it into the flour until you have a mixture that resembles fine breadcrumbs or sand.

Add the eggs and the piloncillo syrup (which should be almost at room temperature by now) and mix with your hands until you have a golden-brown dough. This is a slightly sticky dough, but don't worry, it's totally normal. Don't overwork the dough – as soon as you can form the dough into a ball, wrap it in cling film and refrigerate it for 30 minutes. This will firm up the dough and make it much more manageable to roll and cut.

While the dough rests, make the egg wash by combining the egg, sugar and salt in a small bowl and lightly beating them. The combination of egg and salt will give you a lighter egg wash, while the sugar will help to caramelise the top of the cookie. Set aside.

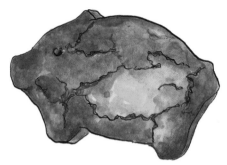

PILONCILLO

There are small variations in flavour between regions, but these cookies are always made in the pig shape and made with piloncillo, which is a form of crystallised sugar made by heating sugarcane juice in conic moulds until it crystalises. Piloncillo is quite a complex-tasting sugar, sweet with an almost smoky, treacly flavour that is wonderfully rich. You can buy piloncillo in my shop, Picado, but you can also substitute it with very dark demerara sugar. But because the sugar is not as flavoursome as piloncillo, I would add 2 tablespoons of molasses or treacle to the mix to enhance it.

Preheat the oven to 180°C fan. Line two baking trays with non-stick baking paper.

Get a rolling pin and your piglet cookie cutter and lightly flour a clean work surface. Remove the dough from the fridge and roll it out to a large circle about 2cm thick. Stamp out the cookies using your pig-shaped cookie cutter and transfer them to the lined baking trays. Leave a bit of space between them, as the piglets will expand a little. Refrigerate the raw cookies on the tray for 15 minutes before you bake them. I find that refrigerating the cookies allows them to keep their shape and not overexpand in the oven.

Bake in the oven for 15 minutes, until the cookies are a dark brown colour. The top of the cookies should still feel quite soft, but they will have developed a lovely dark sheen.

Using a spatula or fish slice, immediately transfer the cookies onto a wire rack and let them cool for 15–20 minutes before tucking in – they are a soft, almost cake-like cookie. Once cooled, store in an airtight container for up to five days.

NEW ZEALAND ANZAC BISCUITS

MAKES 24

BRAD BURGESS – ANZAC biscuits (named after the Australian and New Zealand Army Corps) are a Kiwi icon. Contrary to popular belief, these biscuits didn't make their way to the First World War battlefields of Gallipoli but were sent to troops on the Western Front and sold at galas, parades and other public events at home to raise funds for the war effort. They are still made every April to commemorate ANZAC Day, when Kiwis and Australians come together to remember the Gallipoli campaign and all those who have served and sacrificed in conflict and peacekeeping missions. If you drop by the New Zealand Embassy for ANZAC Day, you will find batches in the oven for sharing with our neighbours and the Kiwi community in Ireland.

120g plain flour

80g rolled oats

170g soft brown sugar

up to 90g desiccated coconut (optional)

125g unsalted butter

80g golden syrup

2 tbsp boiling water

½ tsp baking soda

Preheat the oven to 150°C fan. Line two baking trays with non-stick baking paper.

Mix together the flour, oats, brown sugar and coconut (if using) in a large mixing bowl.

Heat the butter, golden syrup and water together in a medium-sized saucepan. When the butter has melted, stir in the baking soda – it will foam up – then stir the melted butter mixture into the dry ingredients. Combine well, but don't overmix.

Roll the dough into balls the size of ping pong balls. (If you drop by the embassy for a visit, make sure to challenge us to a match on the office ping pong table.) Place on the lined trays, spaced a bit apart to allow for spreading.

Bake for 18–20 minutes, until golden brown and to your desired level of crunch. We reckon a nice chewy centre is best so we don't bake for long, but if you like your biscuits to be chunky and crunchy, they will need to cook a little longer. Allow to cool on a wire rack.

Benson, the embassy's Kiwi Labrador, and Murphy, our Golden Retriever who hails from Connemara, insist on a strict quality control process. Nothing gets out of the kitchen without them first giving it the paws up.

NORWEGIAN JAM THUMBPRINT COOKIES
SYLTETØYKAKER

MAKES 18

SIANAÍL SULLIVAN – These cookies were fun and quick to make with my grandmother when I visited her in Norway during the summer and at Christmas, and they always tasted better when we made our own jam too. In Norway, you could always find these cookies at local bake sales and birthday parties. Almonds, sugar and jam – what's not to love?

200g butter, softened

200g caster sugar

2 eggs

2 tsp almond extract

1 tsp vanilla extract

400g plain flour

2 tsp baking powder

150g apricot, raspberry and/or strawberry jam (thick, not runny – homemade is always best!)

Cream the butter and sugar together until pale and fluffy. Add the eggs one at a time, beating well between each addition until light and airy, then mix in the almond and vanilla extracts.

Sift in the flour and baking powder and mix until evenly combined. Form the dough into a ball, wrap it in cling film and chill it in the fridge for 2 hours.

Preheat the oven to 180°C fan. Line two baking trays with non-stick baking paper.

Roll the dough into balls weighing 50g each and place on the lined baking trays, spaced well apart because they will spread a lot when they bake. Using your thumb, make a wide, deep hole in each ball. Fill each hole with the jam.

Bake on the middle rack of the oven for 15–20 minutes, until golden brown. Allow to cool on the trays for 5 minutes, then transfer to a wire rack to cool completely. These cookies freeze well.

PALESTINIAN DATE-FILLED COOKIES
MAAMOUL

MAKES 2 DOZEN

EMAN ALKARAJEH – Maamoul are popular in Middle Eastern countries and communities around the world, especially during the two Eids, al-Fitr and al-Adha. A few days before these two festivals, women gather to help each other prepare these cookies. The smell will be in the air when passing by people's homes and kids will be waiting close to ovens to win the first cookie with their favourite filling. The recipe may vary from province to province, but generally most people will have a big cake stand full of maamoul in the guest room with Arabic coffee pots all during the day of Eid. Children love Eid because they usually have enough maamoul to last the whole week.

500g plain flour

250g ghee or unsalted butter, softened

½ tsp baking powder

100g caster sugar

5 tbsp milk

FOR THE SUGAR SYRUP:

50g caster sugar

2 tbsp water

FOR THE FILLING:

300g date paste, roughly chopped

1 tbsp ghee or unsalted butter, softened

1½ tsp ground aniseed

1½ tsp ground fennel

TO DECORATE:

icing sugar

First, make the sugar syrup by heating the sugar and water together in a small saucepan over a medium heat until the sugar has dissolved. Set aside.

Beat the flour, ghee or butter and baking powder together for 5 minutes, until it's the texture of breadcrumbs.

In a separate bowl, mix together the sugar and 50g of the sugar syrup – you might have a little left over, which you can discard. Add this to the flour mixture along with the milk and beat until it comes together into a dough. Cover the bowl with cling film and chill in the fridge for 30 minutes.

Preheat the oven to 180°C fan. Line two baking trays with non-stick baking paper.

To make the filling, mix the date paste with the ghee or butter, aniseed and fennel – it might be easiest to do this with your hands, as the date paste is quite thick. Using 1 teaspoon of the filling at a time, roll into small balls – you will use these for stuffing the cookies.

Divide the dough into small pieces (a little larger than the size of a golf ball or 40g) and roll into balls. Working with one ball of dough at a time, flatten the ball into a disc and form it into a small cup. Put a ball of date paste into the cup, then smooth the dough around it until the date filling is completely enclosed (we like to make ours with more filling than dough). You can use a traditional maamoul mould to add a pattern to the top of the cookie or you can make your own pattern with the tip of a small sharp knife. Repeat with the remaining dough and date paste.

Put the stuffed cookies on the baking trays, spaced about 3cm apart. Bake on the middle shelf of the oven for 10–12 minutes, until light golden. Remove from the oven and allow to cool on the trays for 5 minutes, then transfer to wire racks to cool completely.

To serve, dust the cooled maamoul with icing sugar.

PERSIAN RICE COOKIES
NAN-E BERENJI

MAKES 4 DOZEN

SUSAN GOLROO – These cookies remind me of my childhood in Iran, when we travelled to Shiraz in the summer – this sweet comes from that region. I still make these cookies on Naw-Rúz (the Bahá'í New Year on 21 March), but they are also eaten all year round. I remember my family getting together to make these cookies and many others. I showed my grandchildren how to make these and they are very good at it – now they love them too.

4 egg yolks

850g rice flour

1½ tsp ground cardamom

225g unsalted butter, melted

2 tbsp finely chopped pistachios

FOR THE ROSEWATER SYRUP:

300g caster sugar

120ml water

60ml rosewater (or orange juice)

½ tsp lemon juice

To make the syrup, bring the sugar and water to the boil in a saucepan. Boil for only 2 minutes, then remove the pan from the heat and stir in the rosewater and lemon juice. Leave to cool.

Put the egg yolks in a medium-sized bowl and whisk until they're creamy, then whisk in the rosewater syrup.

In another bowl, stir together the rice flour and ground cardamom, then add the melted butter. Mix well for a few minutes, until it's the texture of large breadcrumbs, then add the egg yolk and syrup mixture and mix until it comes together into a dough that no longer sticks to your hands. Cover the bowl with cling film and chill in the fridge for 2–3 hours, until firm.

Preheat the oven to 180°C fan. Line two baking trays with non-stick baking paper.

Roll the dough into balls the size of a walnut. Place on the lined trays, leaving 5cm between them. Make patterns on the top of the cookies by pressing down with the tines of a fork or by using the edge of a small spoon to make a star. Sprinkle over the pistachios.

Bake in the oven for 12–15 minutes. The bottom of the cookies should be a light golden brown when they are done, but the cookies themselves should still be white. Allow to cool on the trays before you move them to a wire rack to cool completely.

POLISH ROSE JAM COOKIES
KOŁACZKI

MAKES 4 DOZEN

PETER SZTAL – These cookies are one of my first childhood memories. I close my eyes and I'm transported to our country garden in Poland and my Granny Wanda, who had a huge hunchback, picking wild roses to make the rose jam. I remember her battered old wicker basket, the tall grass, chickens running around, long summer days, a cookie and a glass of milk straight from the cow after the evening milking.

225g cream cheese, softened

225g unsalted butter, softened

110g caster sugar

1 tbsp vanilla extract

½ tsp almond extract (optional)

¾ tsp fine sea salt

1 egg

355g plain flour

1 jar of rose jam or your favourite jam

FOR DUSTING:

65g plain flour

65g icing sugar, plus extra

Beat together the cream cheese, butter, sugar, vanilla extract, almond extract (if using) and salt until light and fluffy. Add the egg and beat well.

Add the flour and mix until it just comes together into a sticky dough. Spread out a large piece of cling film on your countertop, then tip the dough out onto it, wrap it up and form it into a disc. Refrigerate for at least 2½ hours.

Preheat the oven to 180°C fan. Line two baking trays with non-stick baking paper.

To dust the cookies, whisk together the flour and icing sugar. Working with one half of the dough at a time, roll it out into a rectangle, dusting it in the flour and icing sugar mixture as much as needed, until it's 5mm thick. Cut the dough into 6cm squares and transfer to the lined baking trays.

Spoon about ½ teaspoon of jam on the centre of each square of dough and spread it diagonally in a straight line. (Don't overfill them or the cookies won't stay closed.) Fold together the two opposite corners of the square that don't have the jam and press very firmly to close so that the cookie doesn't pop open while baking.

Bake in the oven for about 20 minutes, until just golden brown. Allow to cool for 5 minutes on the trays, then transfer to a wire rack to cool completely. Dust with icing sugar before serving.

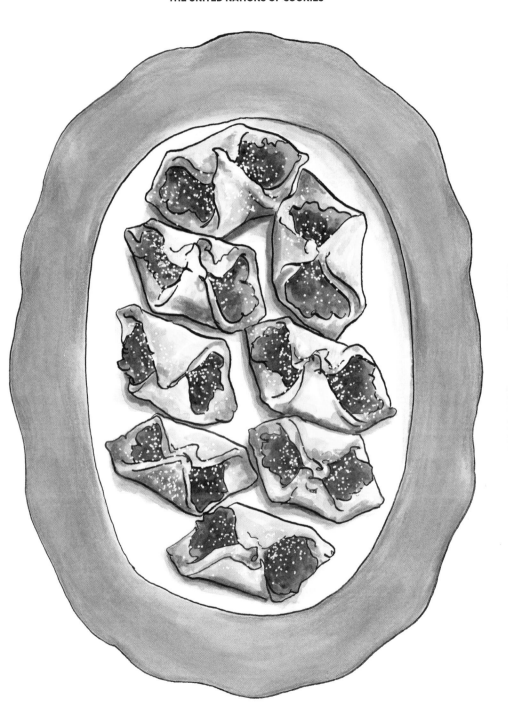

SOMALIAN BISCUITS
BISKUD

MAKES 8 DOZEN

IFRAH AHMED – In Somalia, old women have these biscuits with coffee in the morning. For everyone else, biskud are most often eaten at weddings, Eid, celebrations or as a special treat. You often get a small box of biskud and other sweets to take home with you from a wedding. During Ramadan, you look forward to having these biscuits to break your fast – when I was younger, we'd go to our neighbours' house during Eid and they'd give us these. The traditional shape is a long rectangle with lines on top. In Somalia you can get a special attachment to make this cookie shape by pressing the dough through a meat grinder, but a cookie press fitted with any shape you like is just fine too – flowers are also popular.

190g unsalted butter, softened

200g caster sugar

2 large eggs

1 tsp vanilla extract

500g plain flour

1½ tsp baking powder

½ tsp ground cardamom

Preheat the oven to 180°C fan.

Cream the butter and sugar together until light and fluffy. Add the eggs one at a time, beating well after each addition until fully incorporated and smooth, scraping down the sides of the bowl. Stir in the vanilla.

In a separate bowl, sift the flour, baking powder and ground cardamom together and stir to combine, then add to the wet ingredients and mix just until it all comes together into a dough.

Transfer the dough into a cookie press fitted with whatever shape you like. Push out the cookies directly onto two unlined baking trays.

Bake in the oven for about 15 minutes, until they are light golden brown on top. Leave to cool for a few minutes on the trays before moving onto a wire rack to cool completely. Store in a large glass jar or airtight container and serve with coffee.

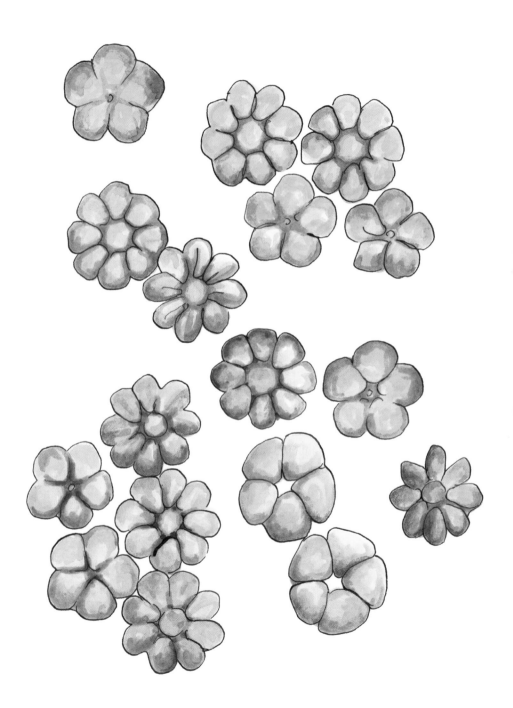

SOMALIA

IFRAH AHMED

Ifrah Ahmed has been supporting UNHCR since 2014 and is now a High-Profile Supporter. Ifrah was born in Somalia and fled the outbreak of war in 2006 at the age of 17. She escaped traffickers and was granted asylum in Ireland. Since settling in Ireland, she has devoted her life to helping eradicate female genital mutilation (FGM) and to providing integration support to newly arrived youth migrants and refugees from Africa in Ireland.

In 2010, Ifrah established the United Youth of Ireland, an NGO that provides support to young immigrants and refugees in establishing businesses, assisting them in settling in Ireland and educating young people about the importance of human rights. Having been a victim of FGM, Ifrah established the Ifrah Foundation in Ireland in 2010, where she advocates for the eradication of FGM in Somalia. In 2012, she succeeded in the establishment of legislation banning the practice in Ireland.

Film has been a central tool in Ifrah's advocacy work. In January 2020, the film *A Girl from Mogadishu*, based on Ifrah's childhood, premiered at the Edinburgh Film Festival. The film is about her life living in a refugee camp in Somalia, where she was born and subjected to FGM and then trafficked as teenager. She was eventually given political asylum in Ireland. The film was awarded both the Audience and Jury Prize at the Semaine de Cinema Britannique, the World Cinema Audience Award at the Mill Valley Film Festival and the Cinema for Peace Award for Female Empowerment at the 2020 Berlin Film Festival

In 2018, Ifrah made a short documentary about a 10-year-old girl who bled to death after undergoing FGM. The documentary went viral, resulting in Somali parents taking their daughters who had undergone FGM to hospitals. Ifrah appeared in the UNHCR six-part series *Too Much Pain: The Voices of Refugee Women* in 2014.

Ifrah has passionately advocated against Tahriib (the practice in which young people regularly embark on the hazardous journey to Europe via human smugglers), including in an interview with Somali Cable TV, where she spoke about the importance of raising awareness of the dangers of Tahriib. She expressed how heart-breaking it is to 'listen to a mother's cry for the loss of her son in such a treacherous journey'. In 2017, Ifrah participated in the UNHCR campaign Dangerous Crossings, which raised awareness about the risks in crossing to and through Yemen from Somalia.

FILM HAS BEEN A CENTRAL TOOL IN IFRAH'S ADVOCACY WORK. IN JANUARY 2020, THE FILM *A GIRL FROM MOGADISHU*, BASED ON IFRAH'S CHILDHOOD, PREMIERED AT THE EDINBURGH FILM FESTIVAL.

SYRIAN SESAME & PISTACHIO COOKIES
BARAZEK

MAKES 18

HAIFA AND SAMI AL JAMOUS – These biscuits are one of the most traditional Syrian sweets. Every family is keen to have this treat during special events like Eid al-Fitr after Ramadan and also Eid al-Adha. We'd buy the ingredients from shops that would stock large amounts of them during Ramadan, as people start buying the ingredients before Eid. Of course all these sweets are available to buy from shops, but we preferred to make our own at home, as every family member has a part in making them. One person makes the dough, another shapes the barazek, someone else sets the pieces in special trays and one is an expert at baking them. We have so many special memories of preparing these biscuits with our families.

110g unsalted butter, softened

80g icing sugar

1 egg

1 tsp vanilla extract

190g plain flour

½ tsp baking powder

a small pinch of fine sea salt

TO DECORATE:

50g sesame seeds

1 tbsp runny honey

50g pistachios, finely chopped

Cream the butter and icing sugar together until pale and fluffy. Add the egg and vanilla and mix again until well combined.

Sift the flour, baking powder and salt together, then gradually fold into the butter and sugar mixture, being careful not to overmix. Cover the bowl with cling film and chill the dough in the fridge overnight.

Preheat the oven to 180°C fan. Line two large baking trays with non-stick baking paper.

Mix the sesame seeds and honey together in a small bowl and set aside. Put the pistachios in a separate bowl or on a plate.

Break off 1 tablespoon portions of the dough and roll into balls. Press one side into the pistachios and the other side into the sesame and honey mix.

Space the barazek 2cm apart on the lined trays. Bake in the oven for 15–20 minutes, until golden brown.

Remove from the oven and allow to cool on the trays for 10 minutes, then transfer to a wire rack to cool completely. Serve with mint tea.

SYRIA

THE AL JAMOUS FAMILY

Ten years into the Syrian crisis, Lebanon remains the country hosting the largest number of refugees per capita in the world. Roughly half the size of Munster, its population has risen by 1.5 million as Syrians began seeking safety there from the onset of the war. Nine in every 10 Syrian refugees now live in extreme poverty and half of the refugee population is food insecure.

Resettlement is a life-saving tool for many refugees in the country, particularly now as the national economic situation deteriorates dramatically. Ireland has responded to the need by pledging to welcome 2,900 refugees between 2020 and 2023.

In 2019, Jess travelled to Lebanon, where she met with the Al Jamous family, who had been selected for resettlement to Ireland. The family are from Da'el near Daraa in southern Syria, which was the centre of the unrest that led to the beginning of the war in Syria in 2011.

Sami, his wife Haifa and their three children – Mohamad Habib (16 years old), Mahmoud (14 years old) and Maria (11 years old) – fled to Lebanon in 2013. They were living in a one-bedroom apartment in Bir Hassan, in southern Beirut. Sami, who worked as a florist in Beirut, was looking forward to the opportunity to find peace and for their children to get a good education.

'Sami had said, all I want is the kids to ride a bicycle up and down the street,' Jess says. 'When I visited them in Birr a year or so later, they were on their bikes in their school uniforms. Haifa was baking and their faces had completely changed. They were so happy.'

'SAMI HAD SAID, ALL I WANT IS THE KIDS TO RIDE A BICYCLE UP AND DOWN THE STREET. WHEN I VISITED THEM IN BIRR A YEAR OR SO LATER, THEY WERE ON THEIR BIKES IN THEIR SCHOOL UNIFORMS. HAIFA WAS BAKING AND THEIR FACES HAD COMPLETELY CHANGED. THEY WERE SO HAPPY.'

TURKISH COFFEE COOKIES

MAKES 3–4 DOZEN

AHMET DEDE – The smell and taste of these cookies were an important part of growing up, as my mother often made these for my father after the work week. They remind me of family time together: me, my two brothers, Mam and Dad. I love making these for my own family and friends now.

6 egg yolks

320g caster sugar

280g unsalted butter, softened

130g olive oil (weigh your oil for a more accurate result)

500g strong white flour

2 tbsp Turkish coffee powder or espresso powder

2 tsp baking powder

Beat the egg yolks and sugar in a stand mixer fitted with the paddle attachment. Add the butter and beat to combine, then gradually add the olive oil and beat again.

Mix together the flour, coffee powder and baking powder, then add to the wet ingredients and mix just until it comes together into a dough. The dough could be firm or quite soft depending on how soft your butter was.

Bring the dough together into a disc (or keep it in the bowl if it's too soft), then wrap it in cling film and chill in the fridge for at least 3 hours, until firm.

Preheat the oven to 160°C fan. Line two baking trays with non-stick baking paper.

Roll the dough out until it's 5mm thick and stamp out into any shape or design you like. Place on the lined baking trays, spaced a little bit apart. Bake in the oven for 10–12 minutes, until the cookies are starting to firm up, keeping in mind that they will firm up more as they cool. Allow to cool on the trays for 5 minutes, then transfer to a wire rack to cool completely.

VENETIAN BUTTER COOKIES
BURANELLI

MAKES 4 DOZEN

ENRICO FANTASIA – These were my favourite cookies when I was a child – and they are still my favourite. They bring me back to my childhood, to afternoons spent in my granny's kitchen watching her cooking and baking. They are typical of my hometown, Venice. It was a feast every time they were on the table, but I particularly loved them for breakfast, dipped in my milk. I don't have much time to do all the baking I'd love to do nowadays, but whenever I'm in Venice I buy them from the local bakery.

250g plain flour

125g caster sugar

a pinch of fine sea salt

100g unsalted butter, diced and softened

zest of 1 lemon

3 egg yolks

2 tbsp milk

1 tsp vanilla extract

Put the flour, sugar and salt in the bowl of a stand mixer fitted with the paddle attachment and mix to combine. Add the butter, then mix until it's the texture of breadcrumbs. Add the lemon zest, egg yolks, milk and vanilla and mix just until it comes together into a stiff dough. (Alternatively, you could do all of this by hand.)

Form the dough into a ball, wrap it in cling film and chill it in the fridge for 30 minutes. If you leave it in the fridge overnight, you'll need to take it out about half an hour before you start making the cookies to make the dough pliable enough to work with.

Preheat the oven to 180°C fan. Line two baking trays with non-stick baking paper.

Pinch walnut-sized pieces off the ball of dough. Roll the dough between the palms of your hands or on the countertop until you get a short, fat log about the thickness of your little finger and measuring about 12cm long. Form into an S shape and place on the lined baking trays, spaced apart.

Bake in the oven for 10–12 minutes, until golden brown. Let the cookies cool on the trays for a few minutes so that they firm up a little, then transfer them to a wire rack to cool completely.

VENEZUELAN EGG COOKIES
GALLETA DE HUEVO

MAKES 12 LARGE COOKIES

MARLON JIMENEZ-COMPTON – These Venezuelan cookies are called galleta de huevo, which means egg cookie. However, it is worth clarifying that eggs aren't included in the ingredients – they are called egg cookies because their colour and shape remind us of an egg yolk. My mammy would give me a coin to buy one or two cookies when she didn't make them herself, as it was cheaper to buy them than to buy the ingredients to make them. These cookies bring back happy memories of my childhood, drinking milk and eating this cookie in particular. They were served at special occasions, but they were also part of our everyday life.

600g self-raising flour

25g baking powder

50g unsalted butter, diced and softened

250g caster sugar

250ml full-fat milk

2 tsp yellow food dye

1 tsp vanilla extract

Mix together the flour and baking powder, then rub in the butter until the mixture resembles coarse breadcrumbs.

Put the sugar, milk, yellow food dye and vanilla in a small saucepan over a medium heat and heat it just a little, until the sugar has dissolved. Add this to the flour and butter mixture and mix it all together to bring it together into a dough. Form the dough into a ball, wrap it in cling film and rest it in the fridge for at least 30 minutes.

Preheat the oven to 170°C fan. Line two baking trays with non-stick baking paper.

Cut the dough in half. Working with one half at a time, roll out the dough until it's 1–2cm thick. Stamp out into circles using a cookie cutter, scone cutter or the rim of a glass and put on the lined baking trays, spaced a little bit apart. Repeat with the other half of the dough.

BAKER'S NOTE

These big, soft, fluffy cookies aren't too sweet – they actually reminded us of scones and like Marlon says, they're perfect with a cup of tea.

Bake in the oven for 20 minutes, until nicely risen and slightly golden around the edges. Let them settle on the trays for 30 minutes before you have your galletas de huevo with a nice glass of milk or a cup of tea.

YEMENI FESTIVE COOKIES
KA'AK AL-EID

MAKES 2 DOZEN

SARA ALTHABHANEY – Ka'ak Al-Eid are like a cross between brioche and a biscuit and they aren't very sweet (in fact, my preference is for no sugar at all). When I was young, I enjoyed making them at home with my aunties or at the neighbours'. Each ka'ak is unique – it has to be shaped and the edges twisted by hand, which felt like some kind of artistic skill.

Ka'ak Al-Eid are home baked – you can't find them in shops, cafés or restaurants. They are traditionally served to guests and only during the Eid (feast) at the end of the fasting month of Ramadhan, Eid al-Adha and at the end of Hajj, the pilgrimage to Mecca, though some families might now serve them on other special occasions. These cookies remind me of my childhood in Yemen – as kids, we liked to dip the ka'ak in sweet, fragrant, milky tea.

150ml lukewarm milk

½ tsp fast action dried yeast

800g plain flour

2 tbsp icing sugar

½ tsp fine sea salt

270g butter, diced and softened

2 eggs

2 egg whites

TO DECORATE:

2 egg yolks

1 tbsp milk

nigella seeds

sesame seeds

Put the warm milk in a measuring jug and stir in the yeast. Leave for 10 minutes to let the yeast foam up.

Mix together the flour, sugar and salt in a large bowl. Add the butter and either using a stand mixer fitted with the paddle attachment or your fingertips, work in the butter until the mixture resembles coarse breadcrumbs. Add the milk and yeast mixture along with the two whole eggs and the two egg whites.

If you're using a stand mixer, switch to the dough hook attachment and knead on a medium speed just until everything comes together into a smooth dough or knead by hand, but either way, take care not to overknead. Cover the bowl with a clean tea towel and leave to rise for 30 minutes in a warm, draught-free place.

Preheat the oven to 190°C fan. Line two baking trays with non-stick baking paper.

Pinch off 50–60g portions of the dough (roughly the size of a large egg) and roll into a ball between the palms of your hands, then flatten each ball into a disc. You can leave them as flat discs, but if you want to create the decorative edge, then flatten all around the edge even more so that

they look almost like ravioli, with a bump in the middle. Using your thumb and forefinger, pinch the edge and twist it towards you to create the decorative edge, repeating this all the way around the disc to create overlapping twists. Place on the lined trays, spaced a little bit apart.

Whisk the egg yolks and milk together, then brush the tops of the cookies with this egg wash. Sprinkle over a small pinch of nigella and sesame seeds on top of each one.

Bake in the oven for 20–25 minutes, until golden brown. Allow to cool on a wire rack, then eat with strong, sweet, milky Yemeni cardamom tea.

YEMEN

SARA ALTHABHANEY

Sara is a forensic science student in GMIT in Galway. She fled the war in Yemen when she was 13 with her mother, sister and brother, seeking safety in Ireland, where they were granted asylum.

After more than six years of conflict, Yemen remains the world's largest humanitarian crisis, with over 4 million people forced to flee their homes inside the country.

Nevertheless, the decision to leave was not one Sara and her family took lightly. 'It's a question of safety,' Sara says. 'You are travelling to an entirely different continent with the possibility that you will never see your family again.'

While food plays an important role in communities around the world, this is even more so for people forced to flee to other countries.

'Having that little bit of home is such a big thing. My mom really enjoys making food; it makes her proud. Being able to create certain food is very close to your heart.' This is even more so in the Arab world, Sara says, where people spend hours producing dishes. 'It is not unusual having to wake at 5 a.m. to get something ready for lunch. It's such a big thing. It holds communities together.'

WHILE FOOD PLAYS AN IMPORTANT ROLE IN COMMUNITIES AROUND THE WORLD, THIS IS EVEN MORE SO FOR PEOPLE FORCED TO FLEE TO OTHER COUNTRIES.

CONTRIBUTORS

KHATIRA HASSANPOUR
AFGHANISTAN
Previously an Afghan refugee living in Iran, Khatira arrived in Ireland in 2018 to be reunited with her husband, Majid. Having completed her master's degree in translation studies in Iran, she hopes to one day pursue her PhD in the topic here in Ireland. Khatira is passionate about literature and loves to write short stories and poetry.

ALICE JARY
BRITAIN
Alice is the chef and co-owner of Rúibín restaurant and bar in Galway. She grew up in Norfolk and has spent most of her adult life in Galway. She has a passion for local and seasonal produce, for cooking with influences from different cuisines and cultures, and for bringing people together through food.
📷 @ruibingalway

HANNAH O'DONNELL
AMERICA
Hannah was born in Massachusetts but her entire family moved to Ireland in 2002. With a background in acting and theatre, she thinks the worlds of food and acting share a lot of similarities, such as the importance of trust, being prepared and a touch of drama.
📷 @crazyred199

JANINE KENNEDY
CANADA
Janine met her Irish partner while they were both living in South Korea and they are now raising their three small daughters on the family's dairy farm in Tipperary. Janine cooks and writes for *Irish Country Living* and is obsessed with local food, sustainable farming and rural life, though a big piece of her heart remains in the tiny Nova Scotian community where she grew up.
📷 @siucrashack

FABIANO MAYOR
BRAZIL
Fabiano was born in São Paulo, Brazil. After working in IT, in 2007 he decided to study culinary arts. He moved to Ireland in 2015 and consulted for many restaurants until he got the opportunity to open Sugarloaf, a traditional Brazilian bakery in Dublin.
📷 @sugarloafdublin

MICKAEL VILJANEN
FINLAND
Born in Sweden but raised in Finland, Mickael is one of only a few chefs in Ireland to have been awarded two Michelin stars. He is the chef-patron at Chapter One in Dublin, previous to which he was the executive chef at the Greenhouse restaurant.
📷 @mickaelviljanenchef

MARISSA MENELAOU
GREECE

Marissa loves creating, cooking and documenting new recipes and her jars are filled with creative treats. Cooking is what Marissa calls productive mindfulness. She is an avid food talker and shares her recipes at www.marissa.co. She captures her meals, new ingredients and places visited on Instagram.

@themarissa.co

YVETTE VAN BOVEN
HOLLAND

Yvette is a critically acclaimed culinary writer, cook, illustrator and TV presenter with her own show on Dutch television. Yvette illustrates and designs all her books herself. She works closely with her husband, photographer Oof Verschuren. Together with their dog Hughie, they divide their time between Amsterdam and West Cork.

@yvettevanboven

KWANGHI CHAN
HONG KONG

Born in Hong Kong, Kwanghi moved to Buncrana, Donegal, when he was eight years old. After training in his family's traditional Chinese restaurant and takeaway, he has gone on to work in in Michelin-starred kitchens, his own street food truck and everything in between. He now runs his Bites by Kwanghi restaurants and ChanChan Asian Sauces.

@kwanghic

MILIE MATHEW & SANTOSH THOMAS
INDIA

Milie and her husband, Santosh, run 3 Leaves, the Michelin-recommended Indian restaurant in Blackrock, Dublin. They started as a tiny stall in Blackrock Market, preparing Indian food that was lovingly cooked and served with the warmest service and never-ending smiles. Milie also works as a cancer nurse with the Irish Cancer Society.

@3leavesblackrock

SUSAN GOLROO
IRAN

Susan was born in Iran. In 1984, she fled Iran along with her husband and three children because of religious persecution of the Bahá'ís there. They came to Ireland as refugees and settled in County Sligo and her children now have families of their own. Susan recently moved to Galway and is very happy there.

ENRICO FANTASIA
ITALY

Enrico has been importing wines to Ireland since 2005. A native of Venice, he works as a private chef in France and Italy, feeding Hollywood actors and European aristocracy. In a previous life he played the French horn in the Gran Teatro La Fenice Orchestra in Venice and in a future life he will do a lot more fly-fishing.

@grapecircus

TAKASHI MIYAZAKI
JAPAN

Takashi trained extensively in fusion teppanyaki cooking before leaving Japan for the Emerald Isle. As the first cherry blossoms opened in 2015, so did his celebrated Japanese takeaway in Cork City, Ichigo Ichie. Word quickly spread about this showcase restaurant for Takashi's treasure box of Japanese food using the best of Irish seasonal ingredients.

@miyazaki_cork

EMILIJA JEFREMOVA
LITHUANIA

Emilija grew up by the beautiful Baltic Sea in Klaipėda, Lithuania, but has been living in the West of Ireland for the last 15 happy years. She is a professional photographer and camera operator who still has strong ties with her home country and family.

@emjcamera

SHAMZURI (SHAM) HANIFA
MALAYSIA

Chef, businessman and broadcaster, Sham moved to Carrick-on-Shannon in 2000, going from general kitchen work to head chef and owner/co-owner of a number of establishments. Sham embodies the Malaysian society that he grew up in, with Chinese and Thai influences from his maternal side and Indian and Malay influences from his paternal side.

@sham__hanifa

LILY RAMIREZ-FORAN
MEXICO

Mexican cook, storyteller, food writer, shopkeeper and lover of all things Irish, Lily is the founder of Picado Mexican Pantry and the author of Blasta Books #1: Tacos.

@lily_ramirezforan

BRAD BURGESS
NEW ZEALAND

Brad opened Aotearoa's Embassy in 2018 and is New Zealand's first resident ambassador to Ireland. Prior to that he held positions in Malaysia and the UK and led trade negotiations for New Zealand. He reckons he is close to mastering the ANZAC biscuit, but all other recipes are a definite work in progress.

@nzinireland

SIANAÍL SULLIVAN
NORWAY

Based in the wild west of Ireland, Sianaíl and his Norwegian mother own a small country grocer where Sianaíl handles the bakery. He taught himself most of what he knows – sleeping in the bakery as a child before school most days of the week probably helped!

@sullivangrocer

64

EMAN ALKARAJEH
PALESTINE

Co-founder of award-winning Izz Café in Cork and mother of four, Eman was raised in a big Palestinian family where connecting with food traditions and skills were routine daily habits. Eman learned her mother's and grandmothers' skills and has added her own modern ones.

@cafeizz

PETER SZTAL
POLAND

Peter hails from Poland but we like to claim him as an honorary Irishman. He landed on our shores in 2002 and after stints working in nightclubs, banking and corporate catering, he went out on his own with a small unit in Dublin's first food hall. He met the love of his life, Frank Kavanagh from Donegal, in 2005 and together the pair founded Dublin's first micro roastery, Cloud Picker Coffee.

@cloud_picker

IFRAH AHMED
SOMALIA

Ifrah, a proud Irish citizen, works tirelessly to put an end to FGM in her native Somalia and worldwide. Ifrah has turned her experience as a survivor into the driving force to make a change for this and future generations. You can find out more at IfrahFoundation.org.

@ifrah.foundation

HAIFA AND SAMI AL JAMOUS
SYRIA

Haifa, Sami and their three children left Syria at the start of the war in 2013. They lived in Beirut before arriving in Ireland on the resettlement programme, which UNHCR runs in partnership with the Irish government. Sami, who worked as a florist in Beirut, was looking forward to the opportunity to find peace and for their children to get a good education.

AHMET DEDE
TURKEY

Ahmet is a Turkish-born chef living in Ireland since 2009. After working in some of the best restaurants in Ireland and Europe, he opened his own restaurant, Dede at the Customs House, in 2020 and achieved a Michelin star within the first year. Ahmet's food is inspired by his heritage, a Turkish fusion spice menu married with local West Cork produce.

@ahmet_dede_

MARLON JIMENEZ-COMPTON
VENEZUELA
Marlon arrived in Ireland in 2003 with only a suitcase and a huge bundle of dreams. He works at Gay Community News and is the co-producer and host of The Marlon Show on Dublin South FM. He is also a member of the Refugee Advisory Board for UNHCR Ireland. Marlon lives to love and loves to live.
@marlife16

SARA ALTHABHANEY
YEMEN
Sara arrived in Ireland from Yemen in 2016 when she was about to turn 14 years old. She started in second year of secondary school in Ballyhaunis, County Mayo while in direct provision there. Her family has since moved to Dublin, while Sara has just completed her second year studying forensic science at the Atlantic Technological University, Galway. Every Eid, Sara helps her mum, Kefa, to prepare ka'ak.

INDEX

Nine Bean Rows Books

23 Mountjoy Square

Dublin, D01 E0F8

Ireland

@9beanrowsbooks

ninebeanrowsbooks.com

**N I N E
B E A N
R O W S**

Blasta Books is an imprint of Nine Bean Rows Books Ltd.

@blastabooks blastabooks.com

First published 2022

ISBN: 978-1-9993799-2-6

Editor: Kristin Jensen

Series artist: Nicky Hooper
nickyhooper.com

Designer: Jane Matthews
janematthewsdesign.com

Proofreader: Jocelyn Doyle

Printed by L&C Printing Group, Poland